I0605811

INTO THE UPSIDE DOWN

First published in 2025 by OH
An Imprint of HEADLINE PUBLISHING GROUP LIMITED

1

Disclaimer:
This book has not been licensed, approved, sponsored, or endorsed by anyone involved in the creation, production or distribution of *Stranger Things* television series.

Cataloguing in Publication Data is available from the British Library

ISBN 978-1-03542-296-8

Compiled and written by: Saneaah Muhammad
Editorial: Victoria Denne
Designed and typeset in Avenir by: Stephen Cary
Project manager: Russell Porter
Production: Arlene Lestrade
Printed and bound in Dubai

Headline's policy is to use papers that are natural, renewable and recyclable products and made from wood grown in well-managed forests and other controlled sources. The logging and manufacturing processes are expected to conform to the environmental regulations of the country of origin.

HEADLINE PUBLISHING GROUP LIMITED
An Hachette UK Company
Carmelite House, 50 Victoria Embankment, London EC4Y 0DZ

The authorised representative in the EEA is Hachette Ireland, 8 Castlecourt Centre, Dublin 15, D15 XTP3, Ireland (email: info@hbgi.ie)

www.headline.co.uk www.hachette.co.uk

INTO THE UPSIDE DOWN

THE LITTLE GUIDE TO STRANGER THINGS

UNOFFICIAL AND UNAUTHORIZED

CONTENTS

INTRODUCTION

Something is coming. A shadow spreads. Lights flicker. A girl with a shaved head runs through the woods. A boy disappears. The world turns upside down – literally.

Since its debut in 2016, *Stranger Things* has gripped audiences with its perfect blend of 1980s nostalgia, supernatural horror and heart-pounding adventure. Created by the Duffer Brothers, this Netflix phenomenon has become one of the most-watched series in streaming history, with Season 4 racking up 1.35 billion hours of viewing time within its first 28 days. The show has won 12 Primetime Emmy Awards and received many award nominations worldwide, including Golden Globes, BAFTAs and SAG Awards.

With its masterful storytelling, unforgettable characters and eerie small-town mysteries, *Stranger Things* weaves a tapestry of suspense.

At its core, the show explores the bond of friendship, growing stronger as the characters face creatures from another dimension. From Demogorgons to Mind Flayers, mixtapes to arcade games and Eggo waffles to Dungeons & Dragons, *Stranger Things* captures the spirit of youth, loyalty and adventure in a world where every shadow hides a secret.

This little book is your gateway to Hawkins, Indiana – a place where friends never lie, bikes outrun government vans and danger lurks beneath the surface. It explores the show's iconic quips, quotes and facts that created a world that captured the attention of millions.

So, turn up the synth, grab your walkie-talkie and get ready to explore the *Stranger Things* universe.

Whatever you do, don't stop running.

CHAPTER ONE

FRIENDS DON'T LIE

In the shadowed town of Hawkins, where secrets lurk and danger whispers, a close-knit crew defies the darkness.

Their bond cuts through deception, standing as a beacon against otherworldly terrors. In a world where nothing is as it seems, one truth remains: friends don't lie.

The unbreakable spirit endures forever.

If we are both going crazy, then we will go crazy together.

”

Mike reassures Will that he's not the only one who feels crazy.

Season 2, Episode 2: "Trick or Treat, Freak"
"Hey Mouthbreathers, We've Got the 45 Best *Stranger Things* Quotes by Character – Everyone From Eleven to Eddie!", parade.com, October 11, 2024

“

What is ‘Friend’?’

”

Eleven learns what a friend is for the first time in her life.

Season 1, Episode 2: “The Weirdo on Maple Street”
"*Stranger Things*: Eleven’s 13 Best Quotes", screenrant.com, May 2, 2023

She's our friend and she's crazy.

”

Dustin scares away their enemies using Eleven as his weapon.

Season 1, Episode 6: "The Monster"
"31 Best *Stranger Things* Quotes of All Time", telltalesonline.com, July 1, 2022

I'm going with my friends. I'm going home.

”

Eleven makes the decision to leave her new crew of supernatural friends to return to Hawkins and help her old friends.

Season 2, Episode 7: "The Lost Sister"
"100 best *Stranger Things* quotes from your favourite characters", legit.ng, February 6, 2023

Friends don't lie. ”

Eleven says the most iconic quote of the show for the first time, expressing that friendship is the most important thing.

Season 1, Episode 7: "The Bathtub"
"Hey Mouthbreathers, We've Got the 45 Best *Stranger Things* Quotes by Character – Everyone From Eleven to Eddie!", parade.com, October 11, 2024

I asked if you wanted to be my friend. And you said yes. You said yes. It was the best thing I've ever done.

”

Mike reminds Will of the day they became friends.

Season 2, Episode 8: "The Mind Flayer"
"31 Best *Stranger Things* Quotes of All Time", telltalesonline.com, July 1, 2022

Mike, don't stop, okay? You're the heart.

Will pushes Mike to keep going, reminding him that he's the heart of their group, keeping them together.

Season 4, Episode 12: "Party Crasher"
"Hey Mouthbreathers, We've Got the 45 Best *Stranger Things* Quotes by Character – Everyone From Eleven to Eddie!", parade.com, October 11, 2024

You're just jealous because I have another older male friend.

Dustin tells Steve that he's no longer the only older friend he has… a reminder that maybe Steve should hang out with friends his own age.

Season 4, Episode 1: "The Hellfire Club"
"31 Best *Stranger Things* Quotes of All Time", telltalesonline.com, July 1, 2022

When I become rich and famous for this one day, don't come crawling back, saying, 'Oh, my God, Dustin, I'm so sorry for being mean to you back in eighth grade.'

Dustin reminds everyone that it's a privilege to be his friend – one day they'll see.

Season 2, Episode 3: "The Pollywog"
"100 best *Stranger Things* quotes from your favourite characters", legit.ng, February 6, 2023

You're all so nerdy, it makes me physically ill.

”

Erica, the youngest of the group, sarcastically criticizes the others.

Season 3, Episode 5: "The Source"
"Hey Mouthbreathers, We've Got the 45 Best *Stranger Things* Quotes by Character – Everyone From Eleven to Eddie!", parade.com, October 11, 2024

We have a lot of rules in our party, but the most important thing is that friends don't lie.

Lucas tells Max the most important rule of their group, hoping to earn her trust.

Season 2, Episode 5: "Dig Dug"
"These Quotes Tell You Everything You Need To Know About Your *Stranger Things* Faves", buzzfeed.com, July 15, 2022

It's very metal what you did. That's all I'm saying.

Eddie admits that he's impressed with Steve's fighting skills.

Season 2, Episode 7: "The Lost Sister"
"Hey Mouthbreathers, We've Got the 45 Best *Stranger Things* Quotes by Character – Everyone From Eleven to Eddie!", parade.com, October 11, 2024

THE MONTAUK PROJECT

Stranger Things was originally called Montauk, based on "The Montauk Project". The alleged government experiment took place in the early 80s and involved kidnapping kids from Long Island to experiment on them.

The show was also supposed to film in Long Island, but this was changed after the realization that it would be too difficult during winter.

The only reason I came in here was 'cause those ladies came in straight after you. Now, I was too ashamed to be the one who stayed behind. But Wheeler right there? She didn't waste a second. Not one second. She just dove right in. Now I don't know what happened between you two, but if I were you, I would get her back. 'Cause that, that was as unambiguous a sign of true love as these cynical eyes have ever seen.

Eddie reveals to Steve that Nancy has feelings for him, after she doesn't hesitate to follow Steve into the Upside Down.

Season 4, Episode 7: "The Massacre at Hawkins Lab"
"All the best quotes from *Stranger Things* Season 4, vol. 1", ew.com, June 1, 2022

There's more to life than stupid boys, you know.

”

Max explains to Eleven that friendships matter as much as relationships.

Season 3, Episode 2: "The Mall Rats"
"Hey Mouthbreathers, We've Got the 45 Best *Stranger Things* Quotes by Character – Everyone From Eleven to Eddie!", parade.com, October 11, 2024

I just didn't look hard enough. But I see you now. I see you.

”

Lucas, to Max, feeling as if he didn't look hard enough to find her – and subtly expressing his feelings for her.

Season 4, Episode 6: "The Dive"
"All the best quotes from *Stranger Things* Season 4, vol. 1", ew.com, June 1, 2022

You can do anything. You can fly. You can move mountains. I believe that, I really do.

”

Mike tells Eleven how he feels about her and how much he believes in her.

Season 4, Episode 9: "The Piggyback"
"31 Best *Stranger Things* Quotes of All Time", telltalesonline.com, July 1, 2022

“I dump your ass!”

Eleven chooses herself over her relationship with a boy, after developing her first strong female friendship with Max.

Season 3, Episode 2: "The Mall Rats"
"*Stranger Things*: Eleven's 13 Best Quotes", screenrant.com, May 2, 2023

You know what I think of you. You're the most incredible person in the world.

Mike reassures Eleven that she is valued and appreciated, as she consistently saves the world.

Season 4, Episode 3: "The Monster and the Superhero"
"All the best quotes from *Stranger Things* Season 4, vol. 1", ew.com, June 1, 2022

This is not yours to fix alone. You act like you're all alone out there in the world, but you're not. You're not alone.

”

Joyce reminds Jonathan that the burden of saving the world and finding his brother is not only on him.

Season 1, Episode 7: "The Bathtub"
"31 Best *Stranger Things* Quotes of All Time", telltalesonline.com, July 1, 2022

“Everything I said about you being a traitor and stuff... I was wrong. I'm sorry.”

Lucas admits to Eleven that he was wrong about his initial judgement of her.

Season 2, Episode 7: "The Lost Sister"
strangerthings.fandom.com

CASTING WITH CARE

Dustin's cleidocranial dysplasia (a condition that affects bone and teeth development) was written in after casting Gaten Matarazzo (the actor who plays Dustin).

Gaten actually has the rare genetic condition and wasn't shy to talk about it.

We never would've upset you if we knew you had superpowers.

”

Dustin, to Eleven, after they discover her special powers – they suddenly grow respect (and a little fear) for her.

Season 1, Episode 2: "The Weirdo on Maple Street"
"Thought-provoking quotes from *Stranger Things*", impertinentremarks.com, April 13, 2017

You can't let these mouth breathers ruin you. Ruin us. I mean, they're nobodies. They're nobodies. And you're a superhero.

Mike reminds Eleven that she's more special than any of the bullies who harass her.

Season 4, Episode 3: "The Monster and the Superhero"
"All the best quotes from *Stranger Things* Season 4, vol. 1", ew.com, June 1, 2022

Well, I call bull on your logic 'cause you're my best friend too.

Mike reminds Dustin that he can have more than one best friend – and that he'll always be one of them.

Season 1, Episode 6: "The Monster"
imdb.com

STRANGE CREATURES

THE DEMOGORGON

First Appearance:

Season 1, Episode 1: "The Vanishing of Will Byers"

Description:

A tall, humanoid creature with elongated limbs and a flower-like head that opens to reveal rows of sharp teeth. It hunts using sound and has immense strength.

Role:

The Demogorgon has an insatiable bloodlust and is responsible for abducting Will Byers and attacking the residents of Hawkins.

Whatever it is, I… I think we should work together. I think it'll be easier if we're… we're a team. Friends. Best friends.

”

Mike, to Will, telling him that they should put the friendship above everything else.

Season 4, Episode 4: "Dear Billy"
imdb.com

I don't know if you can hear this, but… but if you can, I want you to know I'm here, okay? I'm right here. And… I love you. El, do you hear me? I love you.

Mike finally expresses his true feelings for Eleven, although it takes a life-or-death situation to push him to tell her what he really feels.

Season 4, Episode 9: "The Piggyback"
imdb.com

CHAPTER TWO

STRANGE LITTLE CHILD FRIENDS

Hawkins is full of misfits – a superpowered girl obsessed with Eggos, a fast-talking conspiracy theorist, a metalhead with a heart of gold and so many other unique characters, all bringing their own brand of weird.

From Dustin's toothless grin to Steve's legendary hair, their quirks are what make them unforgettable, because in this world, being weird isn't just accepted – it's essential.

Do you wanna be normal? Do you wanna be just like everyone else? Being a freak is the best. I'm a freak.

Jonathan, to Will, making him feel less alone in his weirdness – being a freak is better than being boring!

Season 2, Episode 1: "MADMAX"
"Hey Mouthbreathers, We've Got the 45 Best *Stranger Things* Quotes by Character – Everyone From Eleven to Eddie!", parade.com, October 11, 2024

Touch my butt, I don't care!

”

Dustin proves that he'll do whatever it takes to get through a mission – including having his friends push his butt.

Season 3, Episode 4: "The Sauna Test"
"20 Quotes From *Stranger Things* That Also Work as Pretty Great Advice", menshealth.com, June 8, 2019

We all die, my strange little child friend.

Robin shares her wisdom with her weird, young friends.

Season 3, Episode 7: "The Bite"
"The 8 Best *Stranger Things* Quotes from Seasons 1 to 3", linkedin.com, May 24, 2022

"

When you're different, sometimes you feel like a mistake. But you make her feel like she's not a mistake at all. Like she's better for being different.

"

Will tells Mike how he makes Eleven feel – accepted in a world that sees her as weird.

Season 4, Episode 8: "Papa"
"Hey Mouthbreathers, We've Got the 45 Best *Stranger Things* Quotes by Character – Everyone From Eleven to Eddie!", parade.com, October 11, 2024

You shouldn't like things because people tell you you're supposed to.

”

Jonathan tells his younger brother Will that he's allowed to have his own personality and interests.

Season 1, Episode 2: "The Weirdo on Maple Street"
"31 Best *Stranger Things* Quotes of All Time", telltalesonline.com, July 1, 2022

I'm going as a guy who hates parties.

”

Jonathan attends a Halloween party dressed as... a guy who hates parties.

Season 2, Episode 2: "Trick or Treat, Freak"
"Hey Mouthbreathers, We've Got the 45 Best *Stranger Things* Quotes by Character – Everyone From Eleven to Eddie!", parade.com, October 11, 2024

Nobody normal ever accomplished anything meaningful in this world.

Jonathan shares some of his older brother wisdom.

Season 2, Episode 1: "MADMAX"
"20 Quotes From *Stranger Things* That Also Work as Pretty Great Advice", menshealth.com, June 8, 2019

“

I still highly recommend slapping some juicy pineapple on your pie. Oh, fruit on your pizza is gnarly, you say? Well, I say try before you deny… Hello?

”

Argyle defies anyone to speak out against pineapple on pizza.

Season 4, Episode 4: "Dear Billy"
"Hey Mouthbreathers, We've Got the 45 Best *Stranger Things* Quotes by Character – Everyone From Eleven to Eddie!", parade.com, October 11, 2024

STRANGE BEGINNINGS

Stranger Things is one of Netflix's biggest wins, but this was almost not the case.

Originally, the Duffer Brothers had no plans to pitch to Netflix, but when a new executive started at the company, the brothers had a second chance. The executive was looking for a youth-oriented script, but wanted it to be supernatural.

The Duffers' agent told Netflix about "Montauk", and a pitch meeting with Matt and Ross Duffer was set.

I keep telling him he needs to tame that jungle, but he claims the ladies dig it.

”

Dustin comments on Steve's hairy chest that apparently appeals to the ladies.

Season 4, Episode 6: "The Dive"
"31 Best *Stranger Things* Quotes of All Time", telltalesonline.com, July 1, 2022

Now that you're out of high school, which means you're technically an adult, don't you think it's time you move on from primitive constructs such as popularity?

Dustin schools Steve on the lessons of maturity and acting like an adult.

Season 3, Episode 3: "The Case of the Missing Lifeguard"
"20 Quotes From *Stranger Things* That Also Work as Pretty Great Advice", menshealth.com, June 8, 2019

You know, I'm thinking about calling it *Dustonious pollywogus.*

Dustin thinks of a name for a new supernatural species they have discovered.

Season 2, Episode 3: "The Pollywog"
imdb.com

"

This is Mr. Fibbly. He is a squirrel.

"

Eleven presents her diorama to her class in school… without realizing she could be perceived as weird.

Season 4, Episode 1: "The Hellfire Club"
"*Stranger Things*: Eleven's 13 Best Quotes", screenrant.com, May 2, 2023

Hey, dingus, your children are here again.

”

Robin declares to Steve that his friends are here… his much younger, child-like friends.

Season 3, Episode 1: "Suzie, Do You Copy?"
"Hey Mouthbreathers, We've Got the 45 Best *Stranger Things* Quotes by Character – Everyone From Eleven to Eddie!", parade.com, October 11, 2024

Use the shampoo and conditioner and when your hair's damp, not wet, okay? When it's damp, you do four puffs of the Farrah Fawcett spray.

Steve finally reveals how he styles his iconic hair – with a little help from Farrah Fawcett.

Season 2, Episode 6: "The Spy"
"20 Quotes From *Stranger Things* That Also Work as Pretty Great Advice", menshealth.com, June 8, 2019

I can't believe I will die in a secret Russian base with Steve 'The Hair' Harrington.

Robin despairs over almost dying with Steve and his iconic hair.

Season 3, Episode 6: "E Pluribus Unum"
"100 best *Stranger Things* quotes from your favourite characters", legit.ng, February 6, 2023

Who would I tell? You're my only friend, Jonathan.

Argyle expresses in a vulnerable moment that Jonathan is the closest thing to a friend he has.

Season 4, Episode 2: "Vecna's Curse"
"*Stranger Things*: Argyle's 10 Best Quotes", screenrant.com, June 19, 2022

“Ghost. Halloween.”

Eleven dresses up for Halloween in a costume that makes her completely unrecognizable – a sheet with holes cut out.

Season 2, Episode 2: "Trick or Treat, Freak"
"*Stranger Things*: Eleven's 13 Best Quotes", screenrant.com, May 2, 2023

You keep trying things on until something feels like you.

”

Max encourages Eleven to be herself and find clothes that fit her own personal style.

Season 3, Episode 2: "The Mall Rats"
"20 Quotes From *Stranger Things* That Also Work as Pretty Great Advice", menshealth.com, June 8, 2019

Because you're my best friend! And I would rather be best friends with zombie boy than with a boring nobody.

Jonathan explains to his little brother why he considers him his best friend.

Season 2, Episode 1: "MADMAX"
getyarn.io

Sometimes I think it's just scary to open up like that. To say how you really feel. Especially to people you care about the most. Because, what if... what if they don't like the truth?

”

Will reassures Mike that sometimes it can be difficult to express how you truly feel and show people who you really are.

Season 4, Episode 5: "The Nina Project"
imdb.com

Keep on growing up, kid. Don't let me stop you.

Hopper leaves his heartfelt final words to Eleven in a letter – it is discovered after he is presumed dead.

Season 3, Episode 8: "The Battle of Starcourt"
"The 8 Best *Stranger Things* Quotes from Seasons 1 to 3", linkedin.com, May 24, 2022

Durable. Deadly and reliable. Hear me now – there will be no retreating from Eddie the Banished.

Eddie takes his life back, choosing to fight and refusing to hide.

Season 4, Episode 8: "Papa"
"These Quotes Tell You Everything You Need To Know About Your *Stranger Things* Faves", buzzfeed.com, July 15, 2022

How many children are you friends with?

”

Robin questions Steve on his choice of friends.

Season 3, Episode 2: "The Mall Rats"
"100 best *Stranger Things* quotes from your favourite characters", legit.ng, February 6, 2023

Do you know what this half-baked plan of yours sounds like to me? Child endangerment.

”

Erica seems to be the only one who cares about their safety – ironically, she's the youngest member of their crew.

Season 3, Episode 4: "The Sauna Test"
"100 best *Stranger Things* quotes from your favourite characters", legit.ng, February 6, 2023

THE NETHER

"The Upside Down" was originally called "The Nether" and remained that title on the script.

In the show, Eleven referred to "The Upside Down" and the name stuck, both with fans and on the show.

“Mouthbreather.”

Mike teaches Eleven the commonly used insult in the 80s, describing it as "a dumb person. A knucklehead".

Season 1, Episode 3: "Holly, Jolly"
imdb.com

Okay, I'm warning you right now, I have terrible coordination. It took me six months longer to walk than all the other babies.

Robin confesses that she's not cut out for world-saving adventures – but she'll try her best.

Season 4, Episode 4: "Dear Billy"
"Hey Mouthbreathers, We've Got the 45 Best *Stranger Things* Quotes by Character – Everyone From Eleven to Eddie!", parade.com, October 11, 2024

And you're, like, totally tubular.

Lucas compliments Max in the most 80s way possible.

Season 2, Episode 6: "The Spy"
"*Stranger Things*: Lucas's 12 Best Quotes", screenrant.com, June 13, 2022

Has it ever occurred to you that we don't want to be popular?

”

Mike tells Lucas that being popular isn't his end goal – especially not in the supernatural world they live in.

Season 4, Episode 1: "The Hellfire Club"
"Hey Mouthbreathers, We've Got the 45 Best *Stranger Things* Quotes by Character – Everyone From Eleven to Eddie!", parade.com, October 11, 2024

I may be a pretty shitty boyfriend, but I'm a pretty good babysitter.

”

Steve finally gives in to his role as a glorified babysitter... and he kind of likes it.

Season 2, Episode 9: "The Gate"
"100 best *Stranger Things* quotes from your favourite characters", legit.ng, February 6, 2023

STRANGE CREATURES

THE MIND FLAYER

First Appearance:

Season 2, Episode 3: "The Pollywog"

Description:

A massive, shadowy entity resembling a spider with an ability to control the creatures of the Upside Down. It spreads its influence by infecting hosts.

Role:

It wields control over the Upside Down through psychic connection. Those possessed by the Mind Flayer are known as "the Flayed".

I don't know you that well, kiddo, but I'm betting the fate of the planet that you're one of the good ones.

”

Dr. Owens reassures Eleven that she's a good person, despite her sometimes uncontrollable powers.

Season 4, Episode 3: "The Monster and the Superhero"
"All the best quotes from *Stranger Things* Season 4, vol. 1", ew.com, June 1, 2022

My fingers are like arrows! My arms like iron! My feet like spears! Resist, and I will end you!

Murray prepares himself to enter into a physical fight – using his careful training, of course.

Season 4, Episode 5: "The Nina Project"
"Hey Mouthbreathers, We've Got the 45 Best *Stranger Things* Quotes by Character – Everyone From Eleven to Eddie!", parade.com, October 11, 2024

CHAPTER

THREE

COFFEE AND CONTEMPLATION

Mornings in Hawkins aren't complete without a strong cup of coffee and a moment to process the latest supernatural chaos.

Whether it's Hopper brooding over a case, Joyce piecing together clues or the kids strategizing their next move, deep thoughts and caffeine go hand in hand. Grab a mug – it's time to think.

Well, I'll just write, uh, 'Here Lies Unknown Hero Agent Man'. Yeah. 'Saved Argyle, Jonathan, Will, and Mike from certain death.'

”

Argyle thoughtfully creates a headstone for the unknown man who saved the crew.

Season 4, Episode 5: "The Nina Project"
imdb.com

Could try sticking together at a different house for a change.

Ted, Mike's dad, suggests that the crew find shelter in a different house during a world-ending catastrophe, instead of always theirs.

Season 4, Episode 5: "The Nina Project"
"These Quotes Tell You Everything You Need To Know About Your *Stranger Things* Faves", buzzfeed.com, July 15, 2022

Mornings are for coffee and contemplation.

Hopper refuses to deal with any heavy issues in the mornings – it's his time to relax.

Season 1, Episode 1: "The Vanishing of Will Byers"
"20 Quotes From *Stranger Things* That Also Work as Pretty Great Advice", menshealth.com, June 8, 2019

That's right, she will not be able to resist these pearls.

”

Dustin shows off his new teeth – he suffers from a rare condition that affects bone and teeth growth, so this was his moment.

Season 2, Episode 1: "MADMAX"
"The 10 Best *Stranger Things* Quotes, Ranked", collider.com, August 4, 2024

GLOBAL SENSATION

Stranger Things has captivated audiences worldwide.

Season 4 became the most-watched English-language TV series in its first four weeks, amassing 1.35 billion hours of viewing time within its first 28 days.

It became the second title ever to cross one billion hours viewed.

You do realize that El saved the world twice, right?

”

Mike reminds Dustin that his girlfriend is literally a superhero.

Season 4, Episode 1: "The Hellfire Club"
imdb.com

Why is this wizard obsessed with clocks? Maybe he's, like, a clockmaker or something?

Steve thinks he's cracked the code to their supernatural enemy, though the answer isn't so simple.

Season 4, Episode 5: "The Nina Project"
imdb.com

Okay, it's official. I'm never having kids.

Dustin comes to this hilarious conclusion after running around the mall with Erica, attempting to save the lives of his friends.

Season 3, Episode 7: "The Bite"
"100 best *Stranger Things* quotes from your favourite characters", legit.ng, February 6, 2023

Did you ever think maybe Will went missing because he ran into something bad? And we're going to the exact same spot where he was last seen? And we have no weapons or anything?

Dustin shares his (valid) concerns during their search for Will... to his despair, nobody listens to him.

Season 1, Episode 1: "The Vanishing of Will Byers"
imdb.com

I gotta hand it to you commies, you're committed.

”

Murray comes back with his one-liners and strong grudge against communists – though it seems like a compliment this time.

Season 4, Episode 7: "The Massacre at Hawkins Lab"
"Hey Mouthbreathers, We've Got the 45 Best *Stranger Things* Quotes by Character – Everyone From Eleven to Eddie!", parade.com, October 11, 2024

People don't spend their lives trying to look at what's behind the curtain. They like the curtain. It provides them stability, comfort and definition.

Murray reminds Nancy that not everyone searches for the truth the way they do.

Season 2, Episode 5: "Dig Dug"
"100 best *Stranger Things* quotes from your favourite characters", legit.ng, February 6, 2023

Never tell me the odds.

”

Dustin channels his inner Han Solo and doesn't want to hear his chances of failure – his self-confidence pushes him to only believe in his success.

Season 4, Episode 1: "The Hellfire Club"
"*Stranger Things*: 10 Quotes That Perfectly Sum Up Dustin as a Character", screenrant.com, January 4, 2023

I think it's so sweet that you guys are sticking together like this.

”

Karen, Mike's mother, expresses her admiration for the friendship that the children share.

Season 4, Episode 5: "The Nina Project"
imdb.com

Holy shit, this is trippy.

Robin isn't the only one who is amazed at what she's seeing.

Season 4, Episode 7: "The Massacre at Hawkins Lab"
imdb.com

Do you need to be told everything? You're not a child.

”

Dustin, to Steve, despite being much younger than him – though it seems fitting when all of Steve's friends are children.

Season 4, Episode 5: "The Nina Project"
imdb.com

If a small woman is small enough, she could fit behind a small tree.

”

Argyle shares some interesting, and possibly drug-induced, worldly thoughts.

Season 4, Episode 8: "Papa"
"100 best *Stranger Things* quotes from your favourite characters", legit.ng, February 6, 2023

STRANGE CREATURES

DEMODOGS

First Appearance:

Season 2, Episode 3: "The Pollywog"

Description:

Smaller, quadrupedal versions of the Demogorgon. They grow from slug-like creatures.

Role:

One Demodog is kept by Dustin as a pet named Dart – ironic as it eats his actual pet cat. Dart, and the other Demodogs, are controlled by the Mind Flayer and ultimately attack Hawkins Lab and the people within.

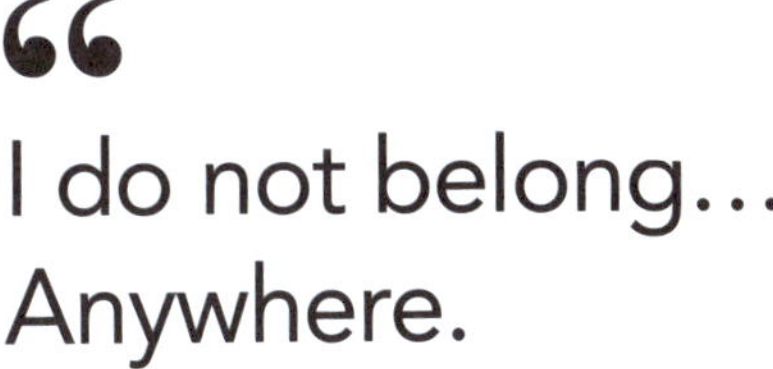

"I do not belong… Anywhere."

Eleven struggles to find her place in this world as a child with supernatural powers.

Season 4, Episode 3: "The Monster and the Superhero"
"*Stranger Things*: Eleven's 13 Best Quotes", screenrant.com, May 2, 2023

You speak of monsters and superheroes. That's the stuff of myth and fairy tales. Reality, truth, is rarely so simple. People are not so easily defined. Only by facing all of ourselves – the good and the bad – can we become whole.

Dr. Benner shares words of wisdom – despite not being trustworthy – about the blurred lines between good and evil.

Season 4, Episode 7: "The Massacre at Hawkins Lab"
"10 Best Quotes From *Stranger Things* Season 4", screenrant.com, May 28, 2022

It's forced conforming. That's what's killing the kids. That's the real monster.

Eddie shares his own fears and the real monsters of the world – much scarier than the creatures trying to kill them.

Season 4, Episode 1: "The Hellfire Club"
"100 best *Stranger Things* quotes from your favourite characters", legit.ng, February 6, 2023

This is the craziest shit I've ever seen in my life. And I've seen some crazy shit.

”

Erica has seen a lot in her 11 years of living... certainly more than any of us.

Season 4, Episode 7: "The Massacre at Hawkins Lab"
imdb.com

If anyone asks where I am, I've left the country.

Mike contemplates running away from his chaotic life and going into hiding.

Season 1, Episode 7: "The Bathtub"
"20 Quotes From *Stranger Things* That Also Work as Pretty Great Advice", menshealth.com, June 8, 2019

That's gotta be a Guinness World Record. Most miles travelled interdimensionally.

Robin wonders about supernatural world records while the others focus on staying alive.

Season 4, Episode 7: "The Massacre at Hawkins Lab"
imdb.com

HONOURS FOR HAWKINS

Incredibly, *Stranger Things* has been nominated for over 250 awards, including 57 Primetime Emmy Awards, four Golden Globe Awards, four Grammy Awards, 13 Saturn Awards, four Critics' Choice Television Awards and countless others.

Of those, the show has won 87 awards, including 12 Primetime Emmy Awards, four Saturn Awards, one Critics' Choice Television Award, one Producers Guild of America Award, one Screen Actors Guild Award and many, many more.

Ask forgiveness, not permission.

”

Nancy decides that some situations have to be acted upon fast, and it's up to them to get it done.

Season 3, Episode 2: "The Mall Rats"
"Hey Mouthbreathers, We've Got the 45 Best *Stranger Things* Quotes by Character – Everyone From Eleven to Eddie!", parade.com, October 11, 2024

Son of a bitch. You're no help at all, you know that?

Dustin tells Mike's dad some harsh truths when he appears useless in a time of desperation.

Season 2, Episode 5: "Dig Dug"
getyarn.io

"Oh, it's the best. I think, yeah, kids dealing with horrifying supernatural forces is to me kind of the best sub-genre in the world. And there's not a lot of it out there, especially stuff that's not targeting kids. I like that a younger audience can enjoy the show, but honestly we wrote the pilot originally to appeal to ourselves entirely and then any hope that it resonates with other people."

Matt Duffer, on creating the show for a younger target audience, but also to appeal to his and his brother's own interests.

"How Steven Spielberg, John Carpenter and Stephen King Influenced *Stranger Things*", ign.com, July 8, 2016

So the good news is I'm pretty sure wooziness is not a symptom of rabies. But if you start having hallucinations or muscle spasms or you start feeling aggressive, like you wanna punch me, let me know.

”

Robin, it seems, may not have a career in medicine...

Season 4, Episode 7: "The Massacre at Hawkins Lab"
Imdb.com

You are beautiful, Nancy Wheeler.

”

Steve expresses his admiration for Nancy – while their relationship changes throughout the show, it's clear his feelings for her always remained.

Season 1, Episode 1: "The Vanishing of Will Byers"
getyarn.io

"Will wanted me to give him some space, so I'm giving him a few feet."

Joyce struggles to give Will his space after his disappearance, so she does it the way any concerned parent knows how.

Season 2, Episode 9: "The Gate"
"100 best *Stranger Things* quotes from your favourite characters", legit.ng, February 6, 2023

Sometimes, your total obliviousness just blows my mind.

”

Dustin can't wrap his head around the way others remain completely unaware, specifically Mike's ignorance.

Season 1, Episode 6: "The Monster"
imdb.com

How many times do I have to be right on the money before you guys just trust me?

Dustin is getting tired of always being right, but never being trusted!

Season 4, Episode 7: "The Massacre at Hawkins Lab"
imdb.com

'The obvious things are not what people observe.' Or... 'Do... Don't observe.' Or... Sherlock Holmes.

Steve tries, and fails, to quote Sherlock Holmes to Nancy to appear smart – after hearing the phrase from his child friend, Dustin.

Season 4, Episode 5: "The Nina Project"
"10 Best Quotes From *Stranger Things* Season 4", screenrant.com, May 28, 2022

And if you need to reach me again… don't.

Murray makes clear that he is no longer on call for world-saving missions.

Season 2, Episode 6: "The Spy"
"*Stranger Things*: 10 Quotes That Perfectly Sum Up Murray as a Character", screenrant.com, August 30, 2022

CHAPTER FOUR

SCIENCE IS NEAT

In Hawkins, science isn't just cool – it's the key to survival.

Whether it's Dustin geeking out over radio waves, Mr. Clarke explaining parallel dimensions or the lab's eerie experiments, the show proves that curiosity and brainpower can unlock the biggest mysteries.

Grab your goggles – it's time to get a little nerdy.

We are nerds and freaks!

”

Dustin reminds Lucas of who they are, and who he's proud to be!

Season 4, Episode 1: "The Hellfire Club"
"Dustin's 10 Greatest Quotes In *Stranger Things*", cbr.com, August 6, 2022

Why do we even need weapons anyway? We have her.

Dustin struggles to find a reason why they need any weapons other than Eleven – she is a girl with superpowers, after all.

Season 1, Episode 3: "Holly, Jolly"
"Thought-provoking quotes from *Stranger Things*", impertinentremarks.com, April 13, 2017

They'd pay, you know, a couple hundred bucks to people like my sister, give 'em drugs, psychedelics. LSD, mostly. And then they'd strip her naked and put her in these isolation tanks... These big bathtubs, basically, filled with salt water so you can float around in there. You lose any sense of, uh, sense and feel nothing, see nothing. They wanted to expand the boundaries of the mind.
Real hippie crap.

”

Becky, Eleven's maternal aunt, explains the experiments that Eleven's mother took part in – possibly explaining why she may have supernatural powers.

Season 1, Episode 6: "The Monster"
"The similarities between *Stranger Things* and IU's involvement in a secret mind control project are CHILLING", archive.thetab.com, November 13, 2017

STRANGE EXPERIMENTS

In *Stranger Things*, Hawkins Lab conducts sinister experiments on test subjects like Eleven, inspired by the real-life MKUltra program.

From the 1950s to the 1970s, the CIA secretly ran MKUltra, testing mind-control techniques using drugs, hypnosis and sensory deprivation – often on unsuspecting people. The goal was to create weapons out of the human mind, but the program was ultimately exposed and shut down.

What's more, the show was filmed in Indiana, and Indiana University was one of the universities that conducted research for the project. Spooky!

I haven't heard from you in a week, and now you want a mathematical equation that you should know to save the world.

”

Suzie isn't shy to show Dustin that she wants to be more than a cog in their bid to save the world.

Season 3, Episode 8: "The Battle of Starcourt"
"100 best *Stranger Things* quotes from your favourite characters", legit.ng, February 6, 2023

Uh, I think a portal to another dimension is going to be pretty obvious.

Dustin, to Lucas, when Lucas questions how they'll know they've arrived at their destination.

Season 1, Episode 5: "The Flea and the Acrobat"
getyarn.io

I am on a curiosity voyage, and I need my paddles to travel. These books... these books are my paddles.

Dustin tries to convince the librarian to allow him to check out as many books as he wants – to help him on his voyage.

Season 2, Episode 3: "The Pollywog"
"20 Quotes From *Stranger Things* That Also Work as Pretty Great Advice", menshealth.com, June 8, 2019

When El took us to find Will, she took us to his house, right? And he wasn't there. But what if he was there? What if we just couldn't see him? What if he was on the other side? What if this is Hawkins and… this is where Will is? The Upside Down.

”

Mike discovers the truth about their missing friend, and the supernatural dimension that will change their lives forever.

Season 1, Episode 5: "The Flea and the Acrobat"
imdb.com

Yes, yes, you're saving the world, I heard you the first time, but Ged is also saving Earthsea and he's about to confront the shadow, so this is Suzie, signing off.

Suzie doesn't have the time to save the boys unless she gets something in return… a duet with Dustin.

Season 3, Episode 8: "The Battle of Starcourt"
imdb.com

"

Part of it was us just getting excited about television and the way it was going, because we grew up as such movie fans, and that was our obsession. [It] was just us going, 'Oh, this is such an exciting arena where we can be part of this generation that's attempting to push the boundaries of what TV is and making it more and more cinematic.' So I think that's where the initial idea came from. And it was us just talking about, 'If we could see any show in the world, what would it be?'

"

Ross Duffer, explaining where the initial idea for the *Stranger Things* came from.

"How Steven Spielberg, John Carpenter and Stephen King Influenced *Stranger Things*", ign.com, July 8, 2016

We're talking about the destruction of our world as we know it.

”

Lucas emphasizes the gravity of the situation they're in.

Season 2, Episode 8: "The Mind Flayer"
"100 best *Stranger Things* quotes from your favourite characters", legit.ng, February 6, 2023

Science is neat, but I'm afraid it's not very forgiving.

Mr. Clarke warns the boys that science has no care for human life.

Season 1, Episode 5: "The Flea and the Acrobat"
"20 Quotes From *Stranger Things* That Also Work as Pretty Great Advice", menshealth.com, June 8, 2019

Joyce says time is funny like that. Emotions can make it speed up or slow down. We are all time travelers if you think about it.

Eleven discovers that time doesn't just tick forward – it can bend with emotions.

Season 4, Episode 1: "The Hellfire Club"
"*Stranger Things*: Eleven's 13 Best Quotes", screenrant.com, May 2, 2023

Once you open up that curiosity door, anything is possible.

”

Mr. Clarke encourages the boys to keep wondering and questioning science.

Season 1, Episode 5: "The Flea and the Acrobat"
"20 Quotes From *Stranger Things* That Also Work as Pretty Great Advice", menshealth.com, June 8, 2019

If she can slam doors with her mind, she can definitely screw up a compass.

”

Lucas is suspicious of Eleven's powers hindering their mission.

Season 1, Episode 5: "The Flea and the Acrobat"
getyarn.io

You telling me Shirley's a human radar detector or some shit?

”

Axel seems dubious about Eleven's powers – but he won't be for long.

Season 2, Episode 7: "The Lost Sister"
getyarn.io

There are parallel universes. Just like our world, but just infinite variations of it.

”

Mr. Clarke confirms the theory of parallel universes – without realizing how much truth there really is to it.

Season 1, Episode 5: "The Flea and the Acrobat"
"*Stranger Things* – Chapter Five: The Flea and the Acrobat", 8flix.com, July 15, 2016

First of all, it's a wrist rocket.

”

Lucas is offended that his friends don't take his slingshot – oops, "wrist rocket" – seriously.

Season 1, Episode 3: "Holly, Jolly"
"Hey Mouthbreathers, We've Got the 45 Best *Stranger Things* Quotes by Character – Everyone From Eleven to Eddie!", parade.com, October 11, 2024

Girls go to science camp?

”

Mike questions Dustin's girlfriend – or maybe he just finds it hard to believe that girls like science too.

Season 3, Episode 1: "Suzie, Do You Copy?"
getyarn.io

There are some things worse than ghosts.

”

Max warns her friends that sometimes the unknown fears are worse than the ones we do know.

Season 4, Episode 2: "Vecna's Curse"
"All the best quotes from *Stranger Things* Season 4, vol. 1", ew.com, June 1, 2022

You guys have been thinking about Hugh Everett's Many-Worlds Interpretation, haven't you?

”

Mr. Clarke is pleasantly surprised that the kids are taking an interest in science… completely oblivious to the dire state their world is in.

Season 1, Episode 5: "The Flea and the Acrobat"
"*Stranger Things* – Chapter Five: The Flea and the Acrobat", 8flix.com, July 15, 2016

Do you know anything about sensory deprivation tanks? Specifically how to build one?

”

Dustin calls his teacher out of school hours to ask a simple, completely harmless question… about sensory deprivation tanks.

Season 1, Episode 7: "The Bathtub"
imdb.com

I say, you're asking me to follow you into Mordor, which, if I'm totally straight with you, I think is a really bad idea. But uh the Shire, the Shire is burning. So Mordor it is.

Eddie describes the situation in the only way he knows how – using pop culture references.

Season 4, Episode 6: "The Dive"
"All the best quotes from *Stranger Things* Season 4, vol. 1", ew.com, June 1, 2022

You know what that is? Melted plastic and microwaved bubble gum.

”

Mr. Clarke explains to his date how special effects are created in movies – ever an enthusiast for science.

Season 1, Episode 7: "The Bathtub"
getyarn.io

Our friend has superpowers, and she squeezed your tiny bladder with her mind.

”

Dustin reveals to his bullies how Eleven used her powers on them.

Season 1, Episode 6: "The Monster"
getyarn.io

There are others who don't believe in you, who think you are the cause. I believe they're wrong. I believe you're the cure.

Dr. Owens reassures Eleven that she can do as much good as she believes she has done bad.

Season 4, Episode 3: "The Monster and the Superhero"
"All the best quotes from *Stranger Things* Season 4, vol. 1", ew.com, June 1, 2022

Why are you keeping this curiosity door locked?

Dustin questions Mr. Clarke about why he refuses to help him with a science question – at ten o'clock on a Saturday.

Season 1, Episode 7: "The Bathtub"
"Hey Mouthbreathers, We've Got the 45 Best *Stranger Things* Quotes by Character – Everyone From Eleven to Eddie!", parade.com, October 11, 2024

Well... you'd have to create a massive amount of energy... to open up some kind of tear in time and space, and then... you create a doorway... like a gate.

Mr. Clarke explains to the boys how to (theoretically) access other dimensions... confirming their theory of the Upside Down.

Season 1, Episode 5: "The Flea and the Acrobat"
"*Stranger Things* – Chapter Five: The Flea and the Acrobat", 8flix.com, July 15, 2016

The Cadillac of ham radios. This baby carries a crystal-clear connection over vast distances. I'm talking North Pole to South.

Dustin shows his friends his new invention, adding at the end (to their surprise), "I can talk to my girlfriend whenever and wherever I choose."

Season 3, Episode 1: "Suzie, Do You Copy?"
"*Stranger Things 3* pays respect to the power and perils of tech", engadget.com, June 30, 2019

STRANGE CREATURES

THE SPIDER MONSTER

First Appearance:

Season 3, Episode 6: "E Pluribus Unum"

Description:

A grotesque, fleshy monster created from liquefied bodies of Mind Flayer-controlled hosts in Hawkins. Its shape loosely resembles the Mind Flayer's shadow in the Upside Down.

Role:

It hunts Eleven and her friends, but loses its connection to the Mind Flayer when the gate to the Upside Down is closed.

We were thinking of more of an evil dimension, like the Vale of Shadows. You know the Vale of Shadows? [An echo of the material plane, where necrotic and shadow magic…] Yeah, exactly. If that did exist, a place like the Vale of Shadows, how would we travel there? Theoretically.

Mike asks his teacher, theoretically, of course, how to travel to a fictional alternate dimension…

Season 1, Episode 5: "The Flea and the Acrobat"
"*Stranger Things* – Chapter Five: The Flea and the Acrobat", 8flix.com, July 15, 2016

You always say we should never stop being curious. To always open any curiosity door we find.

”

Dustin uses Mr. Clark's own words of wisdom against him – so he can unknowingly help them save their friend.

Season 1, Episode 7: "The Bathtub"
imdb.com

CHAPTER FIVE

NEVER STOP BELIEVING

In Hawkins, anything is possible if you just believe.

Whether it's trusting in the impossible, fighting against forces no one can explain or believing in the strength of friendship, the kids prove that faith is a powerful weapon.

Sometimes, the real magic is in holding on to hope – no matter how strange the journey gets.

I'm fine. Okay? I mean, as fine as someone who's hurtling towards a gruesome death can be.

”

Max considers how well she feels in the grand scheme of things.

Season 4, Episode 4: "Dear Billy"
imdb.com

[Promise?] It means something that you can't break, ever.

”

Mike explains to Eleven that a promise can never be broken.

Season 1, Episode 2: "The Weirdo on Maple Street"
"*Stranger Things* – Chapter Two: The Weirdo on Maple Street", 8flix.com, July 15, 2016

I'm not exactly an expert in parenting. But for what little it's worth, I think you did the right thing. The responsible thing. Your children, bless their mischievous souls, they like to get involved. This way, what? They play too much Nintendo, eat too much junk food, smoke some ganja, pound some beers, experiment sexually. I mean really, what's the worst that can happen?

”

Murray reassures Joyce that she's a good parent – especially considering the world-ending circumstances.

Season 4, Episode 3: "The Monster and the Superhero"
tvtropes.org

I kept it open. I kept the door open three inches. I never stopped believing.

99

Eleven reveals that she kept the door open for Hopper – always hoping he would come back.

Season 4, Episode 9: "The Piggyback"
"Hey Mouthbreathers, We've Got the 45 Best *Stranger Things* Quotes by Character – Everyone From Eleven to Eddie!", parade.com, October 11, 2024

A STRANGE SOUNDTRACK

The show's 80s-inspired synth-heavy score, composed by Kyle Dixon and Michael Stein, has become iconic. The soundtrack has also featured classic hits from the 1980s.

Here are some of the most famed:

1. "Should I Stay or Should I Go" – The Clash
2. "Africa" – Toto
3. "Every Breath You Take" – The Police
4. "Running Up That Hill (A Deal With God)" – Kate Bush
5. "Material Girl" – Madonna

Madonna, Blondie, Bowie, Beatles? Music! We need music!

”

Robin desperately tries to find the perfect song to save Nancy from Vecna.

Season 4, Episode 8: "Papa"
imdb.com

If we're trying to avoid angry hicks, maybe we shouldn't go to some store called the War Zone.

Erica gives the crew some good advice on how to stay alive.

Season 4, Episode 8: "Papa"
imdb.com

Steve, if you think that I'm going to spend what is likely the last day of my life in the armpit that is Mike Wheeler's basement, then you're out of your mind. So either take me where I need to go, or you're gonna have to tie me down which is technically kidnapping of a minor and if I live to see another day, Steve, I swear to god, I will prosecute.

Max threatens Steve, the designated babysitter, if he doesn't take her where she needs to go. When Steve responds with "No", Max reveals, "I know a good lawyer."

Season 4, Episode 4: "Dear Billy"
imdb.com

And I know you care about each other very much and that's why it's important that we set these boundaries moving forward so we can build an environment, where we ALL feel comfortable, trusted and open to sharing our feelings. Feelings. Jesus.

Hopper tries to set boundaries between Eleven and Will – of course, trying to control emotional teenagers never works out well.

Season 3, Episode 8: "The Battle of Starcourt"
imdb.com

“

If you believe in this story... Finish it.

”

Mrs. Wheeler gives her daughter, Nancy, some touching advice to keep believing in herself.

Season 3, Episode 4: "The Sauna Test"
"20 Quotes From *Stranger Things* That Also Work as Pretty Great Advice", menshealth.com, June 8, 2019

“

Whatever it is, whatever you do… try not to miss.

”

Max puts all her trust in her friends to keep them all safe.

Season 4, Episode 8: “Papa”
"*Stranger Things*: 15 Best Max Mayfield Quotes", screenrant.com, August 20, 2023

I'm stealthy, like a ninja.

Steve believes in himself a little too much.

Season 1, Episode 1: "The Vanishing of Will Byers"
"100 best *Stranger Things* quotes from your favourite characters", legit.ng, February 6, 2023

“He’s the Starsky to my Hutch.”

Joyce starts to warm up to Murray after all the (life-threatening) adventures they have together.

Season 4, Episode 8: “Papa”
imdb.com

Then you can chop his head off. Stab him in the heart. Blow him up with some explosive Dustin cooks up. I honestly don't care how you put this asshole in his grave.

”

Max gives her friends some encouraging options to fight their enemy, while she keeps him distracted.

Season 4, Episode 8: "Papa"
"*Stranger Things* – Chapter Eight: Papa", 8flix.com, July 1, 2022

It's not easy out there, Nance. I know. People are always saying you can't. That you shouldn't. That you're not... smart enough, not good enough. This world, it... it beats you up again and again until eventually, I... Most people, they just... they just stop trying. But you're not like that. You're a fighter. You always have been.

Mrs. Wheeler gives her daughter some words of confidence: Nancy should be proud of always going against the grain.

Season 3, Episode 4: "The Sauna Test"
"*Stranger Things* – Chapter Four: The Sauna Test", 8flix.com, April 9, 2022

I love you on your good days, on your bad days. I love you with your powers, without your powers. I love you for exactly who you are. You're my superhero.

”

Mike confesses his feeling to Eleven in the hopes that she'll be able to hear him and will fight to stay alive.

Season 4, Episode 9: "The Piggyback"
"31 Best *Stranger Things* Quotes of All Time", telltalesonline.com, July 1, 2022

I'm still… I'm still here. I'm still here.

Max assures Lucas that she's still alive, and he doesn't need to worry.

Season 4, Episode 4: "Dear Billy"
imdb.com

I think we can figure this out. We just gotta open our minds.

”

Jonathan stays positive in yet another world-ending situation, while Argyle stays freaking out.

Season 4, Episode 5: "The Nina Project"
"All the best quotes from *Stranger Things* Season 4, vol. 1", ew.com, June 1, 2022

Never change, Dustin Henderson. Promise me?

”

Eddie keeps Dustin's confidence levels high.

Season 4, Episode 8: "Papa"
imdb.com

“

You can’t just force them apart. I mean, they’re not little kids anymore, Hop. They’re teenagers. If you order them around like a cop, then they’re gonna rebel. It’s just what they do.

”

Joyce reminds Hopper than kids grow up – much to his despair.

Season 3, Episode 1: “Suzie, Do You Copy?”
"*Stranger Things* – Chapter One: Suzie, Do You Copy?", 8flix.com

I am not gonna stop looking for him until I find him and bring him home.

Joyce follows her mother's intuition to keep searching for her son.

Season 1, Episode 4: "The Body"
getyarn.io

You can't spell America without Erica.

Erica proves once again that she is the queen of self-confidence because, of course, the country would not be able to run without her.

Season 3, Episode 4: "The Sauna Test"
"100 best *Stranger Things* quotes from your favourite characters", legit.ng, February 6, 2023

STRANGE CREATURES

VECNA

First Appearance:

Season 4, Episode 1: "The Hellfire Club"

Description:

A humanoid villain with rotting flesh, telekinetic powers and the ability to invade minds. His human form was Henry Creel, also known as One, before being transformed in the Upside Down.

Role:

Vecna is the true mastermind behind the events of Stranger Things, using his powers to kill teenagers and open gates between worlds. He is defeated, but survives… for now.

“

Flay this, you ugly piece of shit.

”

Lucas will always fight off his enemies, but not without insulting them first.

Season 3, Episode 8: "The Battle of Starcourt"
"*Stranger Things*: 10 Quotes That Perfectly Sum Up Lucas as a Character", screenrant.com, July 17, 2022

See how you're leading us here? You're guiding the whole party, inspiring us. That... that's what you do. And see your coat of arms here? It's a heart. And I know it's sort of on the nose, but... but that's what holds this whole party together. Heart. Because, I mean, without heart, we'd all fall apart.

Will reminds Mike of how important he is in the group: he keeps them all together.

Season 4, Episode 8: "Papa"
imdb.com

Make mistakes, learn from them, and when life hurts you – because it will – remember the hurt. The hurt is good. It means you're out of that cave. But please, if you don't mind, for the sake of your old dad, keep the door open three inches.

Hopper reminds Eleven to stay strong through all the struggles, and to never forget him.

Season 3, Episode 8: "The Battle of Starcourt"
"Hey Mouthbreathers, We've Got the 45 Best *Stranger Things* Quotes by Character – Everyone From Eleven to Eddie!", parade.com, October 11, 2024

What's wrong with Winston? He joined the team super late, he's not funny and he's not even a scientist!

”

Lucas needs a little more convincing to believe that Winston is a good Ghostbuster – and a lot more convincing to dress up as him for Halloween.

Season 2, Episode 2: "Trick or Treat, Freak"
imdb.com

You look great, and you're gonna slay 'em dead.

”

Steve gives Dustin a shot of self-confidence after dropping him off at the Hawkins Middle Snowball Winter Dance.

Season 2, Episode 9: "The Gate"
"31 Best *Stranger Things* Quotes of All Time", telltalesonline.com, July 1, 2022

I don't want things to change. So I think maybe that's why I came in here, to try and stop that change. To turn back the clock. To make things go back to how they were. But I know that's naive. It's just not how life works. It's moving, always moving, whether you like it or not. And yeah, sometimes it's painful. Sometimes it's sad. And sometimes, it's surprising. Happy.

Hopper admits that he's afraid to watch Eleven grow up, but that change can be good.

Season 3, Episode 8: "The Battle of Starcourt"
strangerthings.fandom.com

All living organisms develop defence mechanisms against attack. They adapt. They find some way to survive.

”

Dr. Owens explains that it's the natural order of things to adapt and survive.

Season 2, Episode 6: "The Spy"
"100 best *Stranger Things* quotes from your favourite characters", legit.ng, February 6, 2023

I'm tired of being bullied. I'm tired of girls laughing at us.

”

Lucas attempts to become one of the popular kids – oblivious to how this decision will lead him away from his real friends.

Season 4, Episode 1: "The Hellfire Club"
"*Stranger Things*: 10 Quotes That Perfectly Sum Up Lucas as a Character", screenrant.com, July 17, 2022

I didn't run away this time, right?

"

Eddie is proud to have been as brave as his friends... for the first and last time.

Season 4, Episode 9: "The Piggyback"
"Hey Mouthbreathers, We've Got the 45 Best *Stranger Things* Quotes by Character – Everyone From Eleven to Eddie!", parade.com, October 11, 2024

We make our own rules.

Max encourages Eleven to be independent and be her own person.

Season 3, Episode 2: "The Mall Rats"
"*Stranger Things*: 15 Best Max Mayfield Quotes", screenrant.com, August 20, 2023

"Dude, you did it! You won a fight!"

Dustin shares his enthusiasm after Jonathan wins a fight for the first time… after losing many others.

Season 3, Episode 5: "The Flayed"
"100 best *Stranger Things* quotes from your favourite characters", legit.ng, February 6, 2023

Well, when the other dads were teaching their kids how to fish or play ball, my old man was teaching me how to hot-wire.

Murray may not have had a normal childhood, but at least it helps him out on adventures with the gang.

Season 4, Episode 8: "Papa"
imdb.com

You're now faced with the same choice, Jane: go back into hiding and hope they don't find you, or fight and face them again.

Kali, another supernatural human, encourages Eleven to make the choice: hide or fight.

Season 2, Episode 7: "The Lost Sister"
"100 Best *Stranger Things* quotes from your favourite characters", legit.ng, February 6, 2023

“

What I like about the show is that it’s not defined by either one of those descriptions. I like that it has a little bit of everything. To me it’s about these ordinary characters encountering these extraordinary things. We’re following three generations. We’re following the teens, the kids and the adults. Each storyline has a different DNA and a different mood.

”

Matt Duffer, on the main storyline of the show and the different aspects it touches on.

"How Steven Spielberg, John Carpenter and Stephen King Influenced *Stranger Things*", ign.com, July 8, 2016

"Without you, we can't win this war."

Dr. Owens reminds Eleven that she is valuable, even without her powers.

Season 4, Episode 3: "The Monster and the Superhero"
"*Stranger Things 4* Trailer: The Hawkins Gang Goes to War With the Upside Down", variety.com, April 12, 2022

Just talk to me, to your friends! We're right here. I'm right here.

”

Lucas pleads with Max to express her feelings, and reminds her that her friends care for her.

Season 4, Episode 4: "Dear Billy"
"*Stranger Things*: 10 Quotes That Perfectly Sum Up Lucas as a Character", screenrant.com, July 17, 2022

I thought I was put here to pay for what I've done, but I might've been put here for some other reason. Maybe I can, maybe I can still help El, even if it's the last thing I do.

Hopper does all he can to help the kids who constantly save the world.

Season 4, Episode 7: "The Massacre at Hawkins Lab"
"All the best quotes from *Stranger Things* Season 4, vol. 1", ew.com, June 1, 2022

I thought I wanted to be like you. Popular. Normal. But it turns out, normal's just a raging psychopath.

”

Lucas realizes that being unique is better than having seemingly popular friends.

Season 4, Episode 9: "The Piggyback"
imdb.com

Maybe I am a mess, maybe I'm crazy, maybe I'm out of my mind! But God help me, I will keep these lights up until the day I die, if I think there's a chance that Will's still out there!

”

Joyce will stop at nothing to find her son, even if others think she's crazy.

Season 1, Episode 5: "The Flea and the Acrobat"
"These Quotes Tell You Everything You Need To Know About Your *Stranger Things* Faves", buzzfeed.com, July 15, 2022

“

Nothing is going to go back to the way that it was. Not really. But it'll get better. In time.

”

Hopper gives some fatherly advice on moving forward and leaving the past behind.

Season 2, Episode 2: "Trick or Treat, Freak"
"100 best *Stranger Things* quotes from your favourite characters", legit.ng, February 6, 2023

Only love makes you that crazy, sweetheart, and that damn stupid.

”

Police secretary Florence reveals to Nancy that Jonathan has feelings for her.

Season 1, Episode 6: "The Monster"
"Thought-provoking quotes from *Stranger Things*", impertinentremarks.com, April 13, 2017

Bitchin'.

Eleven learns a fun new compliment to add to her very limited vocabulary – at least it's one of confidence.

Season 2, Episode 7: "The Lost Sister"
"Hey Mouthbreathers, We've Got the 45 Best *Stranger Things* Quotes by Character – Everyone From Eleven to Eddie!", parade.com, October 11, 2024

I wish everyone had gotten to know him. Really know him. Because they would've loved him, Mr. Munson. They would've loved him. Even in the end… he never stopped being Eddie. Despite everything. I never even saw him get mad. He could've run. He could've saved himself. But he fought. He fought and died to protect this town. This town that… hated him. He isn't just innocent… Mr. Munson, he's… he's a hero.

”

Dustin ensures that Eddie is remembered in the most heartfelt way – following his sacrifice to help the others.

Season 4, Episode 9: "The Piggyback"
imdb.com

“

I can fight.

”

Eleven will always fight until the very end for her friends – the friendship that kept the world together throughout the entire show.

Season 3, Episode 8: "The Battle of Starcourt"
"*Stranger Things*: Eleven's 13 Best Quotes", screenrant.com, May 2, 2023